CW01272875

Original title:
Crystalline Air

Copyright © 2024 Swan Charm
All rights reserved.

Author: Olivia Orav
ISBN HARDBACK: 978-9908-52-038-4
ISBN PAPERBACK: 978-9908-52-039-1
ISBN EBOOK: 978-9908-52-040-7

Whispers of Light

In the dawn's gentle embrace,
Shadows dance and take their flight.
Golden rays begin to trace,
The earth awakens to the light.

With each beam, a story spun,
Of dreams and hopes that gently rise.
Softly calling, one by one,
To open hearts and clear the skies.

In the twilight, colors blend,
A canvas painted by the day.
Whispers of light, they do not end,
They linger softly, come what may.

Through the night, stars twinkle bright,
Guiding souls on paths unknown.
In their glow, fear takes to flight,
And love finds strength to grow alone.

So let us dance in this sweet glow,
Embracing all that life imparts.
For in the whispers, we will know,
The light within our beating hearts.

Flashes of Clarity

In shadows deep, a spark appears,
A sudden truth, dispelling fears.
A moment held, then lost to time,
Revealing thoughts, pure and sublime.

Through tangled thoughts, a light breaks through,
Illuminating paths, once askew.
Each fleeting glance, a whisper sweet,
A chance to rise, not face defeat.

With every blink, a lesson learned,
The heart ignites, the passion burned.
In darkness, find that glimmer bright,
Embrace the dawn, embrace the light.

Glistening Pathways

In morning dew, the world awakes,
Each blade of grass, a treasure makes.
Beneath the sun, the colors gleam,
A canvas bright, a waking dream.

With every step, the path unfolds,
Stories whispered, secrets told.
The journey calls, both near and far,
Guided onward, like a star.

Through winding trails, and gentle bends,
Nature sings, her soul transcends.
In every turn, a beauty found,
A sacred space, a hallowed ground.

Illusions of Distance

Across the miles, a voice can call,
Yet silence holds, as shadows fall.
What seems so close, slips from our grasp,
An empty echo, a fading clasp.

Through veils of time, we chase the light,
With longing hearts, we brave the night.
Yet in the dark, we find our way,
Through hidden paths, where dreams relay.

Though distance tries, it can't confine,
The bonds we share, forever shine.
In every thought, we bridge the space,
For love endures, a warm embrace.

Dappled Lights

Beneath the trees, the sunlight streams,
In patterned hues, we chase our dreams.
Each gentle sway, a dance of grace,
Shadows play coy, in nature's embrace.

As petals fall, the colors burst,
In every moment, we feel the thirst.
With every breath, the world ignites,
Awakening soul in dappled lights.

In quiet corners, secrets hide,
In whispered breezes, spirits ride.
With open hearts, we seek the glow,
In every step, the magic flows.

Whispers of Shimmering Skies

Beneath the moon's soft glow,
Whispers dance on evening air,
Stars like silver sequins glow,
Telling tales of dreams laid bare.

Gentle breezes weave through night,
Carrying secrets untold,
Flickering with soft delight,
In the darkness, whispers bold.

Clouds like cotton, drift and play,
Painted hues of dawn's first light,
Each dawn brings a hopeful day,
As night surrenders to bright.

In the silence, messages hum,
Random patterns fill the space,
Nature's chorus, sweet and dumb,
Beneath the stars, I find grace.

So let the shimmering skies speak,
Softly guiding, heart's desire,
In their embrace, I feel weak,
Yet embers burn, dreams inspire.

Fragments of Frosted Light

In the stillness, winter's breath,
Whispers sparkle, pure and bright,
Crystals dance in dawn's cold death,
Scattering fragments of light.

Glass-like surfaces reflect,
Each heartbeat caught in icy art,
Silent echoes, hearts connect,
Beauty woven from the start.

Footsteps crunch beneath the weight,
Snowflakes shimmer, softly fall,
Nature's beauty, sharp and great,
In this cold, we hear its call.

Glistening twinkles catch the eye,
While shadows hide the day's retreat,
Frosted wonders fill the sky,
With every chill, new tales repeat.

As we bask in winter's charm,
Finding warmth in icy nights,
Let love's glow, our hearts disarm,
In the fragments of frosted lights.

Celestial Echoes in the Breeze

In twilight's embrace, whispers roam,
Celestial echoes softly play,
Stars abound, a cosmic home,
Guiding dreams until the day.

Gentle winds wrap around me,
Carrying stories from afar,
Each breath hums a melody,
Drawing eyes to every star.

Moonlit paths, they intertwine,
With shadows dancing, fleeting grace,
Here where heart and sky align,
In stillness, we find our place.

Time suspends in twilight's hold,
Where echoes linger, sweet and clear,
Starlit tales of love retold,
Resounding softly, ever near.

Whispered wishes in the night,
Find their way on gentle zephyrs,
Carried far on wings of light,
In celestial echoes, forever.

Glistening Veils of the Morning

Morning breaks with gold and blush,
Softly waking sleepy skies,
Glistening veils of dawn's hush,
Invite the day with bright surprise.

Dewdrops cling to blades of grass,
Each glimmer holds a waking sigh,
A fleeting moment, time won't pass,
As sunlight spills its golden dye.

Birdsong dances through the trees,
A gentle hum of life anew,
In every note, the heart agrees,
With glistening veils, we feel the true.

Light cascades on painted wings,
Painting shadows on the ground,
Every heartbeat gently sings,
In this magic, we're spellbound.

So rise with morning's warming light,
Embrace the day as memories gleam,
In glistening veils, hold on tight,
To whispers of our waking dream.

Nimbus of Hope

In the skies, clouds gather round,
Soft whispers of dreams unbound.
Their shadows dance, glistening bright,
A promise of dawn, breaking night.

Through storms and rain, they provide peace,
A fleeting moment, sweet release.
For in their heart, a light does glow,
Guiding the lost, a nimbus of hope.

With every droplet, life will spark,
Nature awakens from the dark.
A symphony of colors arises,
Reflecting beauty in all sizes.

As the sun breaks through the grey,
Wrapping the world in a warm ray.
An emblem of courage in despair,
The nimbus hugs us, light as air.

Hold tight to hope, let it be known,
In every heart, it has been sown.
With each breath, a wish takes flight,
In the embrace of sparkling twilight.

Luminous Windswept Paths

Underneath the endless skies,
Windswept paths where the spirit flies.
Each turn and twist, a tale to weave,
In nature's arms, we dare believe.

With every stride, the world unfolds,
Stories of warmth, adventure bold.
The light that dances on the ground,
Whispers of wonder all around.

Golden rays through branches stream,
Stirring our hearts with a gentle beam.
Echoes of laughter fill the air,
Luminous hopes, adventures rare.

Step forward, let your worries cease,
Embrace the journey, find your peace.
In the laughter of leaves above,
We find the path that leads to love.

Winds carry dreams where they shall go,
Lifting our hearts, setting them aglow.
Join hands with nature, let's embrace,
The luminous trails that time won't erase.

Shards of Tomorrow

Fragments of dreams, scattered wide,
Whispering secrets, like the tide.
Each shard a vision, bright and clear,
In every heart, they draw us near.

Reflecting hopes, both near and far,
Guiding us like a shining star.
In shadows cast, potential lies,
Awakening truths, where passion cries.

Piecing together what's been lost,
In the pursuit, we count the cost.
Yet through the pain, we start anew,
Shards of tomorrow, glimmering true.

With every choice, a journey starts,
A tapestry woven from many parts.
Embrace the light, let your soul soar,
For tomorrow holds an open door.

Unite the pieces, let them shine,
In every fracture, a grand design.
Together we stand, no longer hollow,
Hope ignites in the shards we follow.

Gleam of the Horizon

As daybreak spills on distant lands,
A gleam of the horizon softly stands.
With colors bold, the canvas wakes,
Awakens dreams that daylight makes.

Across the fields, the light cascades,
Revealing paths where hope pervades.
In every heart, a story glows,
The promise of what tomorrow knows.

Chasing shadows, we start to run,
As dawn unfolds, the battle's won.
Each moment new, a chance to rise,
Beneath the vast, embracing skies.

Let dreams take flight on golden wings,
In the horizon, freedom sings.
The world is vast, and we are free,
To seek the light, to simply be.

So hold the gleam of day so bright,
In every turn, find your true light.
For in the dawn, we start again,
With hearts ablaze, and love to gain.

Elysian Reflections in Stillness

In quiet woods, the shadows sway,
Beneath the trees where whispers play.
The brook enchants with gentle flow,
As time unfolds, serene and slow.

Golden leaves in autumn's breath,
Dance with grace, a soft caress.
Lingering dreams in twilight's glow,
A symphony of peace to show.

Moonlight bathes the path anew,
In silver's touch, the world rings true.
Each step taken, a heartbeat's song,
In Elysian calm, we belong.

Stars adorn the velvet night,
Guiding souls with gentle light.
Among the stillness, spirits soar,
Elysian visions, forevermore.

Misty Prisms of Dawnlight

Morning breaks with soft embrace,
Misty prisms, a fleeting trace.
Sunrise colors, blush and bloom,
Whispers floating, dispelling gloom.

The world awakens, dew-kissed grace,
Nature stirs in a hopeful space.
Reflections dance on silver streams,
Painting life in waking dreams.

Birdsongs echo, sweet and clear,
In the stillness, hearts draw near.
Golden rays through branches weave,
Misty morning, we believe.

Every moment, a fleeting gift,
In dawnlight's glow, the spirits lift.
With every breath, we find our way,
In this tapestry of day.

Lanterns of Ice in Airy Paths

In winter's grasp, the silence glows,
Lanterns of ice where cold wind blows.
Glittering paths through frosted trees,
Whispers riding on icy breeze.

Crystals hang from the branches bare,
Each a story, a light to share.
Underneath a starry quilt,
The air is crisp, the night is built.

Footprints mark the journey bold,
In shimmering silver, the night unfolds.
Softly glimmering in the dark,
Guiding hearts with a gentle spark.

Through airy paths, with love we tread,
Where echoes dance and dreams are fed.
Lanterns shining, a beacon bright,
In the embrace of winter night.

Whispers of Frost

In the hush of dawn's embrace,
Whispers of frost, a feathered lace.
Crystal blooms on windowpanes,
Nature's art in soft refrains.

Each breath visible, a fleeting sigh,
As winter dreams beneath the sky.
Frosted echoes in the air,
Whispers linger, gentle and rare.

Silent woods in a pearl white shawl,
Embracing stillness, a tranquil call.
Every tree, a sentinel,
Guarding secrets, stories swell.

Candles burn in warming homes,
While outside, the frosty gnome roams.
In quiet moments, hearts connect,
With whispers of frost, we reflect.

Celestial Glint

Stars whisper soft secrets,
In the hush of the night,
Awakening dreams afar,
In the cool silver light.

Moments drift like shadows,
Across the velvet sky,
Each twinkling a promise,
None ever asking why.

Galaxies spin their tales,
In colors bright and bold,
A dance of endless wonder,
In the cosmos' hold.

With every shooting gleam,
Hearts rise and fall in sync,
Lost among the heavens,
In stardust we sink.

Celestial stories linger,
On the edge of our dreams,
Connecting us through time,
In the light of their beams.

Veils of Light

Morning breaks like whispers,
In hues of gold and pink,
Veils of light unfurl softly,
As daylight starts to wink.

Through branches dappled lightly,
Sunbeams dance and sway,
Each ray a gentle finger,
Leading shadows away.

The world wakes slowly,
In a warm and tender glow,
Painting dreams in sunlight,
As the soft winds blow.

Branches bow with grace,
To the songs of morning's tune,
While petals turn and shimmer,
Beneath the watchful moon.

Veils of light entangle,
In nature's sweet embrace,
Whispers of dawn's promise,
In each illuminated space.

Translucent Murmurs

Beneath the surface glimmers,
Where thoughts begin to flow,
Translucent murmurs echo,
In the stillness below.

Hidden hopes and wishes,
Bubble up to the light,
Each secret softly shared,
In the depths of the night.

Ripples form like laughter,
A gentle, lilting sound,
As whispers turn to stories,
In quietness profound.

Voices drift like echoes,
Carried on the breeze,
Translucent tales unfurling,
Among the swaying trees.

As twilight paints the world,
In shades of soft delight,
Translucent murmurs linger,
In the heart of the night.

Frosted Reveries

Winter's breath weaves silence,
With a kiss of icy grace,
Frosted dreams upon the ground,
In a shimmering embrace.

Crystals hold the sunlight,
In a dance of gleaming light,
Footprints echo softly,
In the blanket white.

Each flake a whispered secret,
Falling from the sky,
Painting all with wonder,
As the cold winds sigh.

Frosted reveries linger,
In corners of the soul,
Where time stands beautifully,
In a cozy, wintry whole.

As dusk begins to settle,
And the stars make their way,
Frosted dreams awaken,
To welcome in the day.

Radiant Currents

In the depths of the ocean's sway,
Soft whispers of dawn's first ray.
Waves dance gently on the shore,
Echoes of light forevermore.

Colors blend in a vivid swirl,
Nature's magic begins to unfurl.
Life flows free in the embrace,
Of the vast and timeless space.

The sun dips low, casting gold,
Tales of adventure yet untold.
Currents weave through sand and stone,
A journey shared, never alone.

With every heartbeat, rhythms rise,
As stars awaken in the skies.
Radiant paths we choose to roam,
In the currents, we find our home.

Breathe of the Cosmos

Whispers float through the midnight air,
Soft sighs of the universe, fair.
Stars twinkle with secrets to share,
In the silence, dreams laid bare.

Galaxies spin in a dance divine,
Each breath a chance to intertwine.
In cosmic rhythms, hearts unite,
Illuminated by celestial light.

Minds drift far beyond the known,
In the vastness, seeds of thought are sown.
With every pulse, we rise and fall,
Boundless connections weave through all.

From stardust formed, we find our way,
Navigating through night and day.
In this moment, lost in grace,
We breathe together, time and space.

Chilling Harmonies

Whispers of winter fill the night,
As frost adorns the world in white.
Notes drift softly on the breeze,
A symphony among the trees.

Moonlight dances on icy streams,
Casting reflections of silver dreams.
Each heartbeat echoes, calm and clear,
In this chilling atmosphere.

Laughter rings beneath the stars,
As night wraps us in silken scars.
A melody of peace unfolds,
In the warmth, despite the cold.

Harmony begins with every sigh,
Underneath the frosty sky.
Together, we weave a tale so bright,
In the chilling breath of night.

Gleaming Aura

A radiance glows within the soul,
Filling the void, making us whole.
Each moment shines with vibrant hue,
A beacon of hope breaking through.

Sunset hues paint the evening sky,
As whispers of dawn are drawing nigh.
In the golden glow, we find our way,
Glimmers of light lead us to stay.

With every step, the shadows fade,
Guided by light, unafraid.
A gentle spark ignites the heart,
Uniting us, never to part.

In the aura of love, we gleam,
Chasing the echoes of our dream.
Together, we rise, forever bright,
In the gleaming warmth of light.

Ethereal Breath of Dawn

Soft whispers rise with day,
Awakening the silent gray.
Colors spill from nature's hand,
Painting visions across the land.

The sun's embrace, a gentle kiss,
Filling hearts with morning bliss.
Birds take flight in golden light,
A dance of joy, a pure delight.

Shadows fade as warmth unfolds,
Secrets of the night retold.
Every leaf begins to glow,
Touched by warmth, they start to grow.

Clouds drift softly in the sky,
A canvas where dreams learn to fly.
Hope ignites in every beam,
As dawn unfolds, a waking dream.

Embrace the morn, let spirits soar,
With each breath, we live once more.
In the stillness, find your grace,
Ethereal dawn, a sacred space.

Prisms in the Space Between

Hidden gems of light reside,
In the currents, where hopes collide.
Moments passed, yet ever near,
In the silence, truths appear.

Whispers dance on twilight's edge,
Promises made at passion's pledge.
Fractals bend in colors bright,
Painting thoughts in shades of light.

Time weaves tales in subtle threads,
A tapestry of dreams it spreads.
Each heartbeat echoes in the night,
Holding fragments of pure delight.

Invisible paths we tread with care,
Every breath, a silent prayer.
In the chasm, love takes flight,
A prism found in shared insight.

Through the dark, we seek the glow,
In each crack, a chance to grow.
Together we shall find a way,
In the prisms, dreams will stay.

Luminous Currents of Serenity

Underneath the starry veil,
Softened whispers tell a tale.
Moonlit waters gently flow,
Guiding hearts where night winds blow.

Peaceful echoes fill the air,
Floating moments, free from care.
Luminous trails of dreams unwind,
In the stillness, solace find.

Stars above in silent grace,
Shimmer softly in their place.
Every twinkle holds a wish,
In the calm, hearts start to swish.

Embracing night with open arms,
Lost in nature's quiet charms.
Flowing currents, deep and wide,
In this haven, we abide.

Let the waves of tranquil sound,
Wrap you close, securely bound.
In these currents, drift away,
Feel the peace of night and day.

Tranquil Reflections in the Ether

In the stillness of the night,
Mirrors cast a gentle light.
Thoughts like ripples softly glide,
In the ether, hopes reside.

Every breath a measured pause,
Finding comfort in life's laws.
Embers glow with warmth inside,
Guiding us on this quiet ride.

Glimmers dance on water's face,
Echoes of a timeless space.
In reflections, find your place,
Where the heart can slow its pace.

Softly sighs the evening breeze,
Whispered secrets through the trees.
In the calm, we come to see,
Tranquility's sweet decree.

Journey onward, hearts set free,
In this stillness, just to be.
Tranquil thoughts in shadows blend,
Here in ether, woes do mend.

Secrets Amidst the Shimmer

Whispers of night caress the stars,
Shadows hide dreams from the light,
Veils of silence cloak the scars,
In the stillness, secrets ignite.

Moonlit paths weave through the trees,
Footsteps soft on dewy grass,
Nature hums a tune with ease,
Time's embrace makes moments pass.

Glimmers dance on the lake's face,
Echoes resonate with the breeze,
Within this realm, all holds grace,
Mysteries spun with such tease.

Hidden truths in twilight's glow,
Whirling thoughts in quiet streams,
What we sense and don't yet know,
Tales are whispered in our dreams.

Embers fade, yet softly bloom,
Secrets linger, never fade,
Amidst the shimmer, heartbeats loom,
In silence, connections are made.

The Dance of Particles and Hues

In the canvas of the void,
Colors twirl with gentle grace,
Particles form, then are destroyed,
In a waltz through time and space.

Light refracts in joyful arcs,
Shadow's kiss meets vibrant dawn,
The universe ignites its sparks,
As night surrenders to the fawn.

Molecules hum a joyous song,
Twisting fates in cosmic twine,
With every pulse, they glide along,
Painting dreams in every line.

Spectra shift and mirror fate,
In this dance, all nature sways,
Harmony defines the state,
In the rhythm, all life plays.

Gravity's pull and colors bright,
Bring each atom to its place,
Together, they form pure light,
In the cosmos, we find grace.

Feathers of Glimmer in the Breeze

Softly drifting on the air,
Whispers of wings take flight,
Feathers gleam without a care,
Carried forth by day and night.

Colors blend in the soft light,
Glistening against the sky,
A dance of dreams in pure delight,
As the world flows gently by.

Nature's sigh in each light plume,
Grace bestowed in every turn,
With serenity, they bloom,
In the silence, we discern.

Freedom sings in delicate tones,
Riding winds where spirits soar,
Echoes wrap around our bones,
In silence, hearts begin to roar.

The breeze carries stories far,
Whispers lost but not forgot,
In a world spun from each star,
Glimmers of hope, we have sought.

Celestial Fragments

Stars cascade like silver rain,
Fragments scatter, dreams collide,
In this vast and wondrous plain,
Cosmic tales that stars confide.

Time unfolds in layers deep,
Galaxies swirl in tender grace,
In the night, the universe weeps,
In its vastness, we find space.

Whispers twine in the dark's embrace,
Shooting lights carve out their paths,
With every burst, a silent trace,
Of joys and sorrow, love's sweet wrath.

Nebulas paint the skies in hues,
Brushstrokes born from dreams long cast,
Celestial wonders ignite our views,
Each moment flickers, yet holds fast.

Through the cosmos, we drift and roam,
Seeking connections, bonds unbroken,
In this dance, we find our home,
In celestial fragments, unspoken.

Ethereal Breath

In silence where the shadows play,
A gentle sigh comes drifting near.
It carries dreams of night and day,
A whisper soft, a tale to hear.

Between the stars, a lullaby,
With every pulse, it starts to glow.
The cosmos sings a memory,
Of worlds where sacred secrets flow.

Breathe deep the magic in the air,
Feel life's essence intertwine.
Each heartbeat echoes, pure and rare,
A dance of light, a spark divine.

Through hidden realms, the spirits soar,
They weave a tapestry of fate.
With ethereal breath, they explore,
The paths where dreams and hope await.

So listen close, for in the night,
A symphony of stars ignite.
With every moment, pure delight,
Ethereal breath, a soft twilight.

Gossamer Winds

In the glade where fairies dance,
Gossamer winds begin to play.
Whispers carried on chance's glance,
They twirl and spin 'til break of day.

Through the trees, the breezes weave,
Tales of love, secrets untold.
With every rustle, hearts believe,
In magic's grasp, the world unfolds.

Soft petals kiss the morning air,
As sunlight dapples through the green.
With fragile touch, they strip despair,
And paint the world in shades unseen.

Gossamer threads of silver light,
Wrap around the dreams we chase.
They lift our hopes, ignite the night,
With whispers of a warm embrace.

So let the winds guide every heart,
To places where the wild things grow.
In gossamer dreams, we'll never part,
For love's a river, gently flows.

Luminous Shards

In the twilight, fragments shine,
Luminous shards of dreams take flight.
They break the veil of space and time,
Like stardust scattered through the night.

Each shard a wish, a hope, a prayer,
Reflecting truths from deep within.
In crystal light, they find the air,
Revealing paths where life begins.

With every glimmer, stories speak,
Of journeys long and battles won.
In silence, wisdom finds the meek,
And teaches hearts to seek the sun.

Dance with the shards, embrace the glow,
For every spark ignites an art.
With radiant light, let love bestow,
The essence of the human heart.

So gather close, and feel the fire,
Of luminous shards that brightly gleam.
They light the path of pure desire,
And kindle every hidden dream.

Whispering Embers

In the hearth where stories blend,
Whispering embers softly sigh.
They hold the warmth of love, my friend,
A flicker bright beneath the sky.

With every crackle, memories flow,
Of laughter shared and tears once shed.
In glowing light, the past may show,
The journey where our hearts have led.

These embers dance in shades of gold,
Embracing shadows, deep and wide.
They weave a tapestry retold,
Of every joy and every pride.

Each whisper carries tales benign,
Of fleeting moments held so dear.
In every glow, a heart will shine,
Creating warmth, erasing fear.

So let the embers guide our way,
Through darkest nights and brightest dawns.
In whispered tales, we'll find our stay,
As love and hope forever bonds.

Celestial Cascade

Stars spill down in silver streams,
Whispers dance in cosmic dreams.
Galaxies swirl, a vibrant song,
Time holds still, yet moves along.

Nebulae bloom in colors bright,
Painting the canvas of the night.
Stardust floats on gentle breeze,
In silence, I find my heart's ease.

Flickers of Luminance

Faint glimmers spark in shadow's grasp,
Moments slip through fingers fast.
Each flicker holds a story rare,
In the dark, we find our share.

Soft illumination guides the way,
Casting doubts and fears away.
In that glow, hope takes its flight,
Illuminating darkest night.

Aether's Whisper

In the stillness, secrets dwell,
Softened echoes weave a spell.
The breeze carries an ancient voice,
In each sigh, I find my choice.

Through the veil of night it sings,
Cradling dreams on gentle wings.
Every note a tender plea,
Aether's touch, it breathes in me.

Tapestry of Whispers

Threads of silence softly weave,
Stories told for those who believe.
Every murmur, a stitch refined,
In woven hearts, the tales aligned.

Colors blend in twilight's shade,
Embroidered hopes that never fade.
Together, we craft the night,
A tapestry of love and light.

Symphony of the Delicate Atmosphere

Whispers of the wind do sway,
Softly through the trees they play.
Notes of dusk begin to rise,
Painting colors in the skies.

A melody of gentle sounds,
Echoes where the silence bounds.
Stars emerge with tender eyes,
As daylight fades and darkness sighs.

The evening hums a soothing song,
Through the night, it moves along.
Crickets join in harmony,
In this dance of mystery.

Faintest rustle in the air,
Nature's heartbeat, ever fair.
Each note brings a soft embrace,
In this tranquil, sacred space.

Listen close, let worries flee,
In this symphony, be free.
Heartbeats sync with every sound,
Lost in beauty all around.

Flickers in the Daydream

Beneath the canopy of thought,
Fleeting visions gently caught.
Dancing light within the mind,
Revealing wonders left behind.

Shadows play on thoughts of old,
Whispers of stories yet untold.
Each flicker, a spark of grace,
Guiding souls to find their place.

Dreams unfold in silken night,
Stars ignite with tender light.
Visions drift like distant shores,
Unlocking all the hidden doors.

In the pause where silence blooms,
Hope and magic find their rooms.
Time suspended, hearts align,
In this realm, our spirits shine.

Gentle brush of feathered grace,
Mending souls in this embrace.
Flickers guide through endless dreams,
Where life flows in tranquil streams.

A Canvas of Fragile Illumination

Brushstrokes of the morning light,
Kissing petals, pure and bright.
Every hue, a story spun,
In the dance of day begun.

Fleeting shadows softly creep,
Where the earth and cosmos weep.
Fragile truths begin to glow,
Colors blend as feelings flow.

Each canvas tells of fleeting hours,
Captured dreams like blooming flowers.
In this art, we find our way,
Within the light of each new day.

Radiance in tender forms,
Chasing shadows, breaking norms.
A palette rich with whispered sighs,
Illuminating truth, it flies.

Hold the canvas close with care,
Feel the love that wanders there.
In each stroke, let spirit soar,
As life's colors we explore.

Reflections in the Changing Light

Mirrors dance with shifting grace,
Casting shadows, time we trace.
Moments caught in fragile beams,
Whispered secrets, silent dreams.

As the sun dips low and bends,
Light and shadow become friends.
In the twilight, shapes transform,
Echoes of the past, they swarm.

Ripples of a golden glow,
Guide us where the spirits flow.
Each reflection tells a tale,
In the twilight, we set sail.

Fleeting glimpses of the heart,
In each shimmer, worlds depart.
Finding peace in every hue,
In the stillness, we renew.

So let us dance with every shade,
As the daylight starts to fade.
With each transition, life ignites,
Reflections in the changing lights.

Illumination in the Stillness

In the quiet night, stars gleam bright,
Whispers of dreams take gentle flight.
Silvery shadows dance with grace,
In stillness, we find our sacred space.

Minds awaken to the softest call,
Hearts entwined beneath the cosmic sprawl.
Moments linger like the dawn's first light,
Illuminating paths in the soft night.

Thoughts float like leaves on a stream,
Message in silence, a soul's sweet dream.
Each heartbeat, a melody, softly played,
In the hush, our worries fade.

Breathe deeply, feel the sacred air,
Embrace the stillness, let go of despair.
For in this silence, truth may dwell,
Whispering secrets that time cannot tell.

As shadows stretch, the night unfolds,
Stories of wonder silently told.
In the stillness, find your peace,
Let the chaos within you cease.

Glinting Whispers

Amidst the twilight, secrets play,
Glinting whispers guide the way.
Faint glimmers flicker in the dusk,
With every breeze, a sigh, a musk.

Gentle echoes of the past,
In silver threads, memories cast.
Each rustling leaf, a tale untold,
Of love and loss, tender and bold.

Stars shimmer like the eyes of fate,
Glistening softly, never too late.
In the quiet, the world aligns,
With glinting whispers that redefine.

Hold close the moments, let them glow,
In every heartbeat, let love flow.
These whispers linger, a sweet refrain,
Guiding our hearts through joy and pain.

So listen closely as night unfolds,
In every glint, a promise holds.
Whispers of hope, in silence, rise,
In the darkness, a thousand skies.

Dreamy Conversations

As shadows wane and daylight fades,
Dreamy conversations serenade.
Voices like clouds drift and roam,
In the twilight's embrace, we find home.

Words wrapped in warmth, a gentle touch,
In the hush of the night, they mean so much.
With every heartbeat, ideas take flight,
In the realm of dreams, thoughts ignite.

Friends gather close, beneath the stars,
Sharing their hearts, their joys, their scars.
Each story woven with threads of grace,
In the fabric of night, we find our place.

Secrets are whispered, laughter flows,
In this moonlit world, anything goes.
Conversations linger like soft perfume,
Filling the air with love's sweet bloom.

Time becomes fluid, moments blend,
In the dance of stars, our souls transcend.
Dreamy conversations light the way,
Wrapping us close as night turns to day.

Veils of Wonder

In the garden where moments bloom,
Veils of wonder lift the gloom.
With petals soft, secrets unfold,
In nature's heart, stories retold.

Glimmers of magic in the air,
Dancing lightly, without a care.
Colors splash against the sky,
In the silence, the heart dares to fly.

Every whisper, a soft embrace,
Veils of wonder wrap this place.
Embracing dreams that float like mist,
In quiet hours, we can't resist.

Beneath the stars, we close our eyes,
Veils of wonder, endless skies.
With every breath, we feel the sway,
Of magic woven into the day.

As twilight deepens, we surrender,
To veils of wonder, soft and tender.
In nature's embrace, we find our song,
Where fleeting moments will always belong.

Radiant Dances of Hidden Winds

Winds whisper softly through the trees,
Carrying secrets on gentle breeze.
In the twilight, they twirl and sway,
Painting the dusk with shades of gray.

The leaves respond with a rustling song,
Nature's chorus where all belong.
With every gust, the world awakes,
A symphony that fate creates.

Stars peek through the sky's embrace,
In the stillness, we find our place.
Moonlight bathes the dancing night,
Bringing forth dreams, woven tight.

Echoes of laughter, a playful chase,
In the shadows, we find our grace.
Silent moments in between,
Reveal the magic yet unseen.

As dawn approaches, winds will glide,
Holding memories they cannot hide.
Radiant dances in fleeting time,
A story told in rhythm and rhyme.

The Brightness that Lingers

When daybreak spills its golden light,
Hope awakens, dispelling night.
In every corner, shadows flee,
Embracing warmth, we feel so free.

Like petals opening to the sun,
With every heartbeat, life's begun.
Colors burst in vibrant hues,
We find our path, our hearts infused.

Moments stretch, time flows so swift,
Every glance a precious gift.
Memories carved in the morning glow,
The brightness that lingers, always grows.

In laughter shared, in tears that fall,
We stand together, through it all.
Shining brightly, we journey far,
Guided gently by the morning star.

As daylight wanes and shadows creep,
In the heart, these moments keep.
Each fleeting day, a treasure bright,
A tapestry woven of pure light.

Spectres of Light in the Twilight

Twilight dances, a delicate shroud,
Whispers of night, soft and loud.
Spectres of light linger near,
In the fading day, they appear.

Shadows stretch on the cool ground,
Mysteries in silence abound.
Soft glimmers float, then fade away,
Chasing the dream of yesterday.

Stars awaken in velvet skies,
Drawing wishes from hidden sighs.
Every flicker, a story untold,
Unveiling secrets, both brave and bold.

The horizon blushes, a lover's kiss,
In this moment, we find our bliss.
Time pauses, holding its breath,
As darkness dances, mocking death.

In the twilight's embrace, we find
Spectres of light that gently bind.
Guiding hearts through the night so deep,
Together we rise, together we leap.

Veils of Glimmering Silence

In the hush of night, whispers play,
Veils of silence drift away.
Stars shimmer like dreams of old,
In their glow, stories unfold.

The moon weaves tales with silver thread,
Illuminating paths we tread.
Each breath a promise, soft and clear,
In this silence, all draws near.

Glimmers flicker, a dance so sweet,
With every heartbeat, we feel the beat.
In the stillness, the world reveals,
The essence of everything it feels.

In moments caught between the hours,
Nature breathes, unveiling powers.
With every sigh, the cosmos hums,
In glimmering silence, the heart succumbs.

As dawn approaches, the veils unwind,
A tapestry of peace defined.
In the quiet, we find our song,
A love that lingers, forever strong.

Lightborne Whispers of the Cosmos

Stars flicker in the night,
Their secrets softly told,
Galaxies sway and spin,
A tale of ages old.

Comets trail their fiery glow,
Painting paths across the sky,
Each spark a whispered wish,
As dreams in stardust fly.

Nebulas bloom in hues divine,
A cosmic garden's grace,
Among the stellar wonders,
We lose ourselves in space.

Planets dance in silent songs,
With moons as partners bright,
Infinite in their embrace,
An everlasting night.

In the quiet of the void,
Lightborne whispers hum,
Inviting souls to wander,
Till daybreak's songs become.

Echoes in the Whispering Ether

Echoes float on gentle winds,
A serenade of night,
Voices lost in twilight haze,
Where shadows kiss the light.

Whispers curl in the cool air,
Secrets shared with grace,
Each breeze a fleeting moment,
A memory of space.

Stars align in silence deep,
Conversations without sound,
In the heart of stillness,
Infinite truths are found.

Raindrops speak to thirsty soil,
A rhythm soft and sweet,
Nature's symphony unfolds,
In every pulse, a beat.

Through the ether, dreams take flight,
In whispers, we ascend,
With echoes guiding softly,
On journeys without end.

The Veiled Dance of Airborne Crystals

Delicate jewels in the air,
Sparkling in sunlight's gaze,
Crystals dance with graceful flair,
In a kaleidoscope's maze.

Windswept trails of glimmering light,
Whirling in a fluid trance,
Each shard a fleeting insight,
Inviting hearts to dance.

Voids filled with shimmering dust,
A tapestry of refrains,
Within the veils, we trust,
Emerging from our chains.

Clouds cradle these gems with care,
An embrace both warm and pure,
Ethereal threads in the air,
A beauty we can't secure.

In the whispering sky above,
Airborne crystals twirl and play,
Their veiled dance, a sign of love,
That brightens up our day.

Illuminated Dreams in the Blue

In the vastness of the blue,
Dreams take flight on feathered wings,
Illuminated by the sun,
Hope in every heartbeat sings.

Clouds float like whispers soft,
Painting stories in the sky,
Each puff a canvas aloft,
Where fantasies learn to fly.

Oceans reflect the sapphire hue,
Mirroring the dreams we weave,
Waves carry wishes anew,
In the depths, we believe.

As the horizon blurs and blends,
Colors merge in soft embrace,
In the twilight, each heart mends,
And finds its cherished place.

Illuminated dreams arise,
In the calm of evening's glow,
Together under starlit skies,
Through the blue, our spirits flow.

Fragments of Twilight

In the fading light of day,
Shadows dance and sway,
Colors blend in soft embrace,
Leaving traces, a gentle trace.

The stars begin to gleam,
Guiding dreams of silver stream,
Whispers float on evening air,
Promises hidden, always rare.

Mountains sigh in twilight's glow,
Rivers murmur, secrets flow,
Trees bow low to kiss the ground,
In this moment, beauty found.

Twinkling lights in heavens vast,
Echoes of a day now past,
Feelings linger in the breeze,
Captured softly, moments freeze.

As darkness wraps the world in grace,
Hope finds refuge, a sacred space,
With every breath, the night unfolds,
Whispers of twilight, stories told.

Shimmering Whispers

Moonlight spills on silver seas,
Softly stirring whispered pleas,
Gentle waves caress the shore,
Secrets held forevermore.

Stars above, they seem to sigh,
Glimmers sparkling in the sky,
Hearts beat to the ocean's song,
Finding where we all belong.

A breeze dances through the trees,
Carrying sweet memories,
Tales of love and fleeting hours,
Blooming bright like summer flowers.

In the night, dreams come alive,
With shimmering whispers, we thrive,
Cast our worries to the tide,
In this magic, we confide.

Hold these moments in your heart,
Let the serenity impart,
For in whispers, life transcends,
Here, where every journey blends.

Reflection in the Mist

Morning breaks, the fog draws near,
Shrouding all in silence clear,
Mystic shapes begin to rise,
Hidden truths and muted sighs.

A soft touch of dewy grass,
Memories swirl as shadows pass,
In the stillness, echoes play,
Hints of brightness in the gray.

Voices linger, faint and low,
In the mists, where secrets flow,
Moments captured, fragile, bright,
Woven deep in soft twilight.

Chasing dreams through silken air,
Finding warmth is always rare,
Within this veil, we seek to find,
Pieces of a wandering mind.

As the sunlight breaks the haze,
New reflections greet the days,
In the mist, our souls will soar,
Hoping to return once more.

Ephemeral Essence

Life's a whisper, soft and sweet,
Moments fleeting, bittersweet,
Like the petals on their flight,
Fleeting beauty, pure delight.

In the stillness, we remain,
Caught between joy and pain,
Embers glow in twilight's grace,
Every heartbeat, time's embrace.

Stars above, they twinkle bright,
Guiding us through endless night,
As the shadows slowly fade,
Essence lingers, unafraid.

For in this dance of give and take,
We find the memories we make,
Embrace the now, let go the past,
In every moment, love is cast.

As dusk approaches, dreams ignite,
Holding close to what feels right,
Ephemeral, yet deeply known,
In our hearts, we find a home.

Mists of Splendor Taking Flight

In dawn's embrace, the mists arise,
Veils of silver 'neath the skies.
They whisper tales of dreams untold,
A dance of beauty, bright and bold.

From twilight's hush to morning's glow,
The colors mingle, soft and slow.
Each breath of air, a story spun,
Of nature's magic, just begun.

The whispers weave through trees and streams,
A tantalizing thread of dreams.
In every sigh, a secret's shared,
As light and shadow are ensnared.

With wings of wonder, we take flight,
Into the soft, enchanted light.
Engulfed in mists, we lose our ground,
In splendor's grasp, we are unbound.

The Lightness Beneath the Surface

Beneath the waves, a world of grace,
Where light and shadow dance in space.
A glimmer shines, so soft, so clear,
Whispering secrets for those who hear.

Each bubble bursts with joy anew,
A fleeting glimpse of ocean blue.
The currents carry tales of old,
Of treasures lost and dreams retold.

Coral beds like painted skies,
Beneath the waves, all beauty lies.
The colors blend, a soft caress,
In liquid realms, we find our rest.

With every stroke, we find our tune,
A symphony beneath the moon.
In depths so deep, we come alive,
The lightness floats, and we survive.

Hues of the Invisible Realm

In twilight's hush, the colors blend,
A canvas stretched that knows no end.
Invisible hues, a quiet song,
That whispers softly, linger long.

Through shadows cast, and light's embrace,
We find enchantment in this place.
Each shade a story, rich and vast,
From ancient echoes, whispers past.

Glimmers of gold in dusky air,
Paint stories only dreamers dare.
In every outline, forms take flight,
Invisible tapestries of light.

Within the depths of all we see,
Lie sacred truths that set us free.
So let us wander, hearts unfurled,
Through hues unseen, in this strange world.

Enchantment in the Breezy Expanse

Upon the winds, our laughter soars,
In breezy realms, through open doors.
With every gust, a new delight,
An enchanting dance, a joyful flight.

The trees sway gently, with each breeze,
Telling stories, bending knees.
A tune that's played on nature's breath,
In moments shared, we conquer death.

Clouds drift softly, like thoughts of old,
Their tales hold warmth, like sunlit gold.
The sky, a canvas, vast and wide,
With every turn, we take our stride.

In this expanse, our spirits rise,
Carried forth by endless skies.
With hearts aglow in this embrace,
We find our place, our sacred space.

Veils of Glee

In the garden, laughter sings,
Colors dance on gentle wings.
Sunlight weaves through blooming trees,
Whispers carried by the breeze.

Joyful chirps of morning birds,
Echo sweetly, without words.
Beneath the sky, so vast and blue,
Happiness blooms anew.

Every petal, bright and bold,
A story of delight retold.
In this place, our hearts unite,
Veils of glee in pure sunlight.

Gentle streams flow with a song,
Nature's tune, where we belong.
Laughter ripples, clear and bright,
In the warmth of pure delight.

Moments shared, forever free,
Crafting memories like the sea.
Waves of joy, a sweet refrain,
In our hearts, the love remains.

Reflections of Serenity

In still waters, peace does gleam,
Quiet whispers of a dream.
Softly flowing, time stands still,
Echoes linger, calm and will.

Moonlight dances on the lake,
Gentle ripples softly break.
Stars above in silence glow,
Guiding hearts where breezes blow.

In the shade of ancient trees,
Nature hums its melodies.
Every leaf a tale unfolds,
Whispers sweet, as time beholds.

Moments drift like leaves in fall,
Embracing peace, we heed the call.
Under skies of deep azure,
We find solace, sweet and pure.

With every breath, a gift we take,
Finding balance, hearts awake.
A tranquil mind, a soothing stream,
Within us flows a peaceful dream.

Echoes of Luminosity

In the dawn, the light reveals,
Shadows fade, a warmth that heals.
Golden rays touch every face,
Painting hope in every space.

Upon the hills, the colors play,
Guiding hearts through morning's sway.
A symphony of light and grace,
Capturing each fleeting place.

As daylight wanes, the stars appear,
Whispers of the night draw near.
Twinkling jewels in velvet skies,
A lullaby that never dies.

Beneath the moon, we find our way,
Lost in dreams where shadows sway.
In this dance of light and dark,
Echoes spark a lasting mark.

Illuminated paths we tread,
Shining bright, our hearts are fed.
In unity, we shall ignite,
The echoes of our shared light.

Drifting a Dream

On gentle wings, we float away,
To distant lands where shadows play.
Underneath the starlit skies,
Whispers carried, soft goodbyes.

Clouds like pillows, soft and white,
Cradle us in endless flight.
Through the night, where wishes gleam,
Sailing softly down a dream.

Time dissolves in silver streams,
Moments blend, like fleeting dreams.
With every heartbeat, worlds combine,
In this place, your hand in mine.

As dawn breaks, the journey calls,
Into the light, where hope enthralls.
Colors burst, a brand new start,
Drifting dreams within the heart.

Here we find our truest selves,
In stories woven from the shelves.
Boundless skies where spirits soar,
Drifting dreams forevermore.

Notes of Clarity in a Whisper

In the quiet, thoughts collide,
Soft echoes whisper, dreams abide.
The night's embrace, a tender song,
Guiding hearts where they belong.

Each note a thread of fragile light,
Stitching shadows, igniting the night.
With every breath, a chance to see,
Truth revealed, to set us free.

In gentle tones, the world unfolds,
Stories woven, secrets told.
In whispers soft, we find our way,
To brighter paths where hopes can sway.

The heart, a compass tuned to grace,
Navigating through time and space.
In delicate moments, find your tune,
Dance with shadows beneath the moon.

Embracing change, we rise and fall,
The whispered notes, they call us all.
With clarity wrapped in tender sighs,
We journey forth, through endless skies.

The Ether's Gentle Embrace

In the ether, silence sings,
Tender breezes convey soft things.
Stars align in a cosmic grace,
Filling hearts in a warm embrace.

Veils of mist, a calming shroud,
Whispers dance, both soft and loud.
Moonlight spilled on open seas,
Cradled softly by gentle breeze.

With every heartbeat, worlds collide,
In cosmic realms, thoughts abide.
Emotions weave, both wild and free,
Anchored deep in eternity.

Each breath taken, a sacred prayer,
Floating softly in the air.
In the vastness, we find our place,
Touched by the ether's warm embrace.

Moments linger, like whispered dreams,
In twilight's glow, where starlight gleams.
Together we rise, though shadows fall,
In this embrace, we unite all.

A Dance of Frost and Light

Amidst the chill, the world ignites,
A dance unfolds in frosted sights.
The crispness wraps around the air,
As nature hums a song so rare.

Light breaks through the winter's chill,
A golden glow on frost-kissed hill.
Each flake a note of shimmering song,
In this ballet, we all belong.

With every twirl, the shadows play,
Chasing darkness, ushering day.
The trees adorned in glistening art,
Embrace the dance, the beating heart.

In this moment, pure and bright,
Harmony reigns in the dance of light.
Together we swirl, a joyful flight,
In a world transformed, both calm and bright.

The frost, it whispers of change to come,
A promise wrapped in the beating drum.
In unity's step, we dance and twine,
A celebration of love, divine.

Shards of Illumination

Fractured reflections, shards in flight,
Scattered dreams caught in the night.
Each glimmer tells a tale so bright,
Carving paths through darkened sight.

In the chaos, a spark will shine,
Whispered secrets, old and divine.
Illuminating shadows, bold and clear,
Casting light where hearts adhere.

Glinting visions, echoes of hope,
In the fragments, we learn to cope.
Through broken glass, the truth ignites,
In vivid hues, we reclaim our rights.

A tapestry woven with threads of grace,
Radiant paths, a warm embrace.
Shattering limits, embracing the new,
In shards of light, we find our true.

From darkness comes beauty, shining bright,
Illumination reigns, banishing night.
Together we rise, hearts open wide,
In this dance of light, we cannot hide.

Kisses of Celestial Frost

Under the veil of a shivering night,
Stars twinkle softly, pure and bright.
Whispers of dreams in the icy air,
Embrace the chill with tender care.

Frosted petals glint in pale light,
Nature slumbers, wrapped tight in white.
A moment's grace, a silent song,
In the frost's kiss, we all belong.

The moon, a guardian in the sky,
Watches as shadows flit and fly.
Each digital breath, a vaporous tale,
Carried away on the winter's gale.

Branches glisten, adorned with ice,
A fleeting beauty, oh so nice.
Hands entwined, lovers gaze,
Lost in the magic of frozen haze.

Come, feel the chill, a gentle tease,
Kisses of frost in the winter breeze.
Promises made beneath the dark,
Igniting the night with a hopeful spark.

A Palette of Atmospheres

Colors swirl in the dawn's embrace,
Painting visions in the vast space.
Golden rays kiss the horizon,
Awakening the world, a sweet season.

Clouds, a canvas in endless hues,
Whispers of blue, shades of muse.
Crimson sunsets spill and flow,
Crafting a story in every glow.

Gentle winds brush across the skin,
Bringing warmth where dreams begin.
A symphony of tones softly sing,
In the heart of each awakening spring.

Night falls like an artist's hand,
Spreading darkness, yet so grand.
Stars emerge, like dots on a sheet,
Creating wonders that feel so sweet.

A palette rich with every breath,
Life's vibrant strokes, a dance with death.
In every sky, a tale untold,
With every shade, a moment bold.

Silhouettes of Luminous Hope

In the hush of dawn, shadows form,
Casting dreams, both soft and warm.
Figures dance on the edge of light,
Chasing away the remnants of night.

Whispers of wishes ride the breeze,
Carried on currents with effortless ease.
Each silhouette, a promise anew,
Holding the dreams we dare to pursue.

Stars linger, in twilight's embrace,
Guiding the heart to a hopeful place.
In the night sky, we find our path,
Navigating shadows, avoiding wrath.

Hope glimmers like a distant star,
Reminding us just how near we are.
With hearts aflame, we reach above,
Crafting our futures with light and love.

In every journey, shadows may fade,
Yet luminous hope is never betrayed.
As mornings break, and night holds ground,
In every silhouette, love is found.

Radiance on a Breath of Wind

In the gentle stir of the evening air,
Lies a magic both delicate and rare.
Carrying whispers from far and near,
A breath of the cosmos, crystal clear.

Light dances softly on the wings of time,
Kisses the world, like a nursery rhyme.
Every gasp, a secret, a fleeting trace,
Painting the moments of life's embrace.

Veils of dusk unfurl with grace,
Wrapping the earth in soft, warm lace.
The heartbeat of nature, a silent band,
Pulsing in rhythm with a tender hand.

Clouds drift lazily, a serene ballet,
Guiding the sun toward the end of day.
With each caress of the evening gust,
We find our peace, in this we trust.

Radiance gleams on a breath of wind,
Each moment cherished as stories begin.
As dusk embraces the end of light,
Hope ignites in the heart of the night.

Chasing the Dew

Morning light peeks through the trees,
Soft whispers dance upon the breeze.
Glistening droplets on blades of green,
A fleeting world, so fresh, so clean.

Each step I take, the shadows play,
As dew-kissed petals greet the day.
Nature's jewels, they shimmer bright,
A thousand gems, pure delight.

In stillness found, the world awakes,
With every breath, the spirit takes.
Awash in hues of amber glow,
I forge ahead, chasing the dew.

Winds of change whisper through the grass,
In this fleeting moment, I wish to last.
Rays of sun begin to climb,
In this dance of dew, I lose all time.

Oh, how I yearn for mornings dear,
To lose myself, to have no fear.
With every drop, a promise made,
In the beauty of dawn, I wade.

Echoes in the Void

In the silence, shadows creep,
Where memories linger, secrets keep.
A distant whisper, a fading sigh,
In the emptiness, dreams go by.

Crimson skies, where sunsets drown,
In the echoes, I wear my crown.
Faces flicker, then disappear,
In the void, I confront my fear.

With every thought, the silence swells,
In the dark, I craft my spells.
Threads of time, a fragile weave,
In this vastness, I believe.

Stars above like diamonds gleam,
In the void, I chase a dream.
Though surrounded by shadows deep,
I find solace in what I keep.

As echoes fade into the night,
I search for warmth, for guiding light.
And in this dance of endless space,
I find my strength, I find my place.

Shards of Serenity

In tranquil moments, stillness reigns,
Whispers of peace erase my chains.
Gentle sighs in twilight's glow,
Through shards of calm, my spirit flows.

Soft petals fall from trees above,
In the quiet, I feel your love.
Each breath a step toward the light,
Shattered pieces, yet all feels right.

In the chaos, I seek this space,
Fragments shimmer in soft embrace.
Reflections dance on water's face,
A patchwork quilt, an endless grace.

Here in the stillness, I unfold,
The stories of life, both brave and bold.
With every shard, I stitch anew,
In the tapestry of me and you.

As night descends and stars appear,
I gather strength, I cast out fear.
In this realm of serenity,
I find the depth of all I see.

Haze of Dreams

In the mist where echoes roam,
I wander far, I find my home.
Veils of fog, they cloak the night,
In the haze, I seek the light.

Faint whispers call from shadows deep,
In sleepless hours, my secrets keep.
The world unfolds in soft embrace,
In dreams, I float to a sacred place.

Illusions shimmer, fleeting grace,
Each dream a dance, a wondrous chase.
I reach for stars that flicker bright,
In the haze, I take flight.

With every breath, the night's refrain,
Restless thoughts like falling rain.
In the depths, I pave my way,
In the haze of dreams, I long to stay.

As dawn approaches, shadows fade,
I capture moments, the dreams I made.
In this journey, I've come to find,
The haze of dreams, forever entwined.

Celestial Brushstrokes

In twilight's gentle glow, they paint,
Stars scattered, like dreams they faint.
A canvas vast, dark and deep,
Where secrets of the night dare keep.

Whispers of cosmos dance and twine,
Each stroke a mystery, divine.
Galaxies spin with colors bold,
A story of the universe told.

Moonbeams drape the earthly scene,
With hues of silver, soft and keen.
A brush dipped in stardust bright,
Crafts a tapestry of light.

Auroras flare in vibrant hues,
A symphony of morning blues.
Celestial wonders silently nod,
As night surrenders to the dawn's facade.

With every brushstroke, time awakes,
In cosmic rhythms, life remakes.
A masterpiece of night and day,
In celestial realms, we long to stay.

Cascades of Ether

Gentle streams of ether flow,
Through valleys where soft breezes blow.
Dancing light on water's face,
Nature's touch in warm embrace.

Whispers travel on the breeze,
Softened echoes through the trees.
Leaves rustle with secrets untold,
As sunlight weaves its threads of gold.

Cascades tumble, swift and clear,
In every drop, there's life to revere.
Reflections shimmer, fade and sway,
In this fluid dreamland, we play.

Mountains cradle skies so vast,
In tranquil moments, shadows cast.
With every pulse, a heartbeat sighs,
In harmony beneath the skies.

The air is thick with a gentle hum,
In nature's grasp, we find the sum.
Cascades of ether, wild yet tame,
In each moment, we stake our claim.

Waves of Haze

In morning's grasp, dreams softly blend,
Misty tendrils twist and bend.
Waves of haze roll through the day,
In soft gray whispers, spirits play.

The world transformed in veils of light,
Boundless thoughts take endless flight.
A dance of shadows on the ground,
Where silence speaks without a sound.

Hope emerges in the foggy dawn,
As sunlight breaks, the night is gone.
Waves of hazy comfort cling,
A lullaby that life can sing.

Every heartbeat echoes clear,
In the stillness, truths adhere.
Through layered thoughts, we navigate,
These waves of haze, we celebrate.

With each step, the world unfolds,
Mysteries wrapped in stories told.
As shadows fade, the light will blaze,
Awakening life from waves of haze.

Harmonics of Hope

In the quiet of the night, we dream,
Life's symphony begins to gleam.
Every note a whispered tale,
In harmonics, we will prevail.

From shadows deep, melodies rise,
Guided softly by starry skies.
With courage wrapped in gentle sound,
A chorus of hearts begins to pound.

Rhythms pulse in every beat,
A fusion of spirits, strong and sweet.
Together we rise, hand in hand,
In the dance of life, we'll make our stand.

Through trials faced, we find our way,
In the harmonics, come what may.
Hope's delicate tune will always shine,
A beacon bright, our hearts align.

In every struggle, in every fight,
Harmonies echo through the night.
In the fabric of our lives, we weave,
Harmonics of hope, we believe.

Vows of the Breeze

Whispers float on tender air,
Promises made without a care.
Gentle touch of nature's breath,
Binding lives, igniting depth.

Windswept fields where wishes soar,
Carried far to distant shore.
Hearts entwined with each soft sigh,
Vows bestowed beneath the sky.

Leaves respond with rhythmic dance,
Nature sings, a sweet romance.
In every gust, a love letter,
Eternal bonds that grow, not fetter.

Beyond horizons, dreams take flight,
Guided by the stars at night.
In every breeze, a whispered truth,
Revealing love's unyielding youth.

So let us walk where breezes call,
With every vow, we rise, we fall.
In the rhythm of nature's ease,
Our hearts unite in sacred breeze.

Celestial Frost

Stars descend like diamonds bright,
Draping earth in silver light.
Each flake whispers of the night,
In the dance of sheer delight.

Underneath the blanket white,
Dreams awaken, take their flight.
Cold embrace, a gentle kiss,
Wrapped in time, we find our bliss.

Moonlight glints on frozen streams,
Nature weaves our silent dreams.
In the chill, warmth hides away,
As night sways and turns to day.

Frosted fields where shadows play,
Catch the dawn before it sways.
Every moment etched in frost,
In this beauty, we are lost.

Yet as dawn breaks through the haze,
Light ignites the world, ablaze.
From celestial frost we rise,
Carved in love beneath the skies.

Dancing in the Ether

In the space where dreams ignite,
We twirl beneath the stars so bright.
Every breath a spark of flame,
In the dance, we lose our name.

Echoes of our laughter ring,
Floating on a whispering wing.
Gravity bends to our delight,
As we spin through endless night.

Galaxies weave our sacred song,
Binding souls where we belong.
Each movement, a story told,
In the ether, hearts unfold.

Through the void, our spirits soar,
Chasing dreams forevermore.
In the rhythm, time stands still,
In our dance, we find our will.

So let us dance among the stars,
In the twilight, love is ours.
Boundless joy, we freely share,
Dancing in a cosmic prayer.

Shivering Silence

In the hush of night so deep,
Where shadows linger, secrets keep.
Every breath a fragile sigh,
In shivering silence, hearts comply.

Moonlit paths, so softly tread,
Whispers echo where dreams are spread.
In the quiet, fears take flight,
Wrapped in peace, we find our light.

Time suspends in still embrace,
Gentle touch of time and space.
In the stillness, we belong,
Finding strength in silent song.

Stars above, they flicker low,
Marking trails for souls to follow.
In shivering silence, hearts entwined,
A peaceful home within the mind.

Through the dark, we find our way,
Guided by the night's ballet.
In this calm, our fears are tamed,
In shivering silence, love is named.

Soft-Shimmering Horizons

In the morning's gentle glow,
Where dreams and daylight blend,
Soft whispers of the breeze flow,
A new journey to transcend.

Misty shapes at break of dawn,
Colors dance in sweet delight,
Nature's canvas, softly drawn,
A promise held in twilight.

Each horizon invites the soul,
To wander near and far away,
In whispers that make us whole,
Beneath the soft hues of day.

The sun dips low, a golden thread,
Stitching sky with earth's embrace,
To dance on paths where dreams are led,
A shimmered hope we all can trace.

No shadows linger, only light,
As hearts align with what is true,
In soft-shimmering hues so bright,
Horizons speak their secrets too.

Fleeting Moments of Transparency

In twilight's breath, the world fades,
As whispers weave through evening air,
Moments shift in soft cascades,
A glimpse of what we hope to share.

The laughter echoes, lightly draped,
In fragile holds of time's soft thread,
Like morning dew on petals shaped,
These fleeting moments turn our head.

Reflections caught in glassy streams,
A portrait of our hearts' desire,
In every sigh, we chase our dreams,
In fragile flames that never tire.

With every blink, a story told,
In silent words, we find our grace,
Though moments fade, memories hold,
The essence of a fleeting place.

So hold these shadows close and tight,
As laughter dances on the breeze,
In fleeting moments, pure and bright,
We find the depth of life with ease.

Wings of Diaphanous Light

Fluttering softly through the air,
With wings that glisten, faint and pure,
A dance of light beyond compare,
In every flicker, dreams endure.

These gossamer forms glide and sway,
Carrying whispers of the sky,
Each moment feels like a ballet,
Where spirits soar, and hearts comply.

In the embrace of twilight's grace,
They weave a tapestry of peace,
A fleeting touch, a sweet embrace,
In diaphanous light, we release.

Their shimmering trails, a soft gleam,
We chase in hopes of what could be,
Born from the wisps of a dream,
In wings of light, we learn to see.

With every pulse of gentle air,
These whispers turn to songs of night,
Eclipsing sorrow, raising care,
In worlds created by soft light.

The Journey of Twinkling Shards

In the night sky, fragments shine,
Scattered dreams on velvet black,
Each twinkle tells a tale divine,
A journey on a starlit track.

These shards of light, they come alive,
In cosmic dances, bright and bold,
Through whispered wonders, dreams arrive,
With stories waiting to be told.

They weave a path through endless night,
Connecting souls, both near and far,
A silhouette wrapped in soft light,
Believing in the guidance of a star.

Each glimmer holds a secret song,
A promise held in heaven's clasp,
In every blink, where hearts belong,
We find the truth in starlit grasp.

So let us drift where shards collide,
And dance in worlds beyond our sight,
For in this journey, we abide,
In the magic of twinkling light.

Glacial Serenade

Mountains whisper cold tunes,
In the twilight's silver hue.
Ice crystals dance in the night,
While stars twinkle, pure and bright.

Frozen rivers softly flow,
With secrets only they know.
Underneath the moon's soft glow,
Nature's beauty starts to show.

Frosty winds gently sigh,
Telling tales from long gone by.
Echoes in the frozen air,
A symphony beyond compare.

Each flake tells a story old,
In the silence, dreams unfold.
Underneath the winter's veil,
Life's enchantment will prevail.

As dawn brings a warm embrace,
Whispers fade without a trace.
Yet the glacial song remains,
Carried softly through the plains.

Prisms in the Sky

Clouds drift lightly overhead,
Painting colors as they tread.
Sunbeams glimmer, breaking free,
Nature's art for all to see.

Raindrops catch a fleeting light,
Creating rainbows, pure delight.
A spectrum arching far and wide,
In this brilliance, dreams abide.

Wind whispers secrets untold,
In each hue, emotions bold.
The canvas shifts with every breeze,
Awakening the heart to seize.

Time suspended in the glow,
As shadows dance, and colors flow.
In this moment, life takes flight,
In prisms of the morning light.

Hope reflects from every shade,
In this vibrant masquerade.
Together, let our spirits rise,
Beneath the beauty of the skies.

Fractured Light

Shattered beams fall to the ground,
In their chaos, beauty found.
Splinters of the day anew,
Crafting patterns bright and true.

The dance of shadows on the wall,
In their wander, they enthrall.
Memory glimmers where they pass,
In the silence, echoes last.

Each reflection tells a tale,
Of journeys grand, of dreams weail.
A whisper caught on silver threads,
In the light, where mystery spreads.

Fleeting moments, caught in flight,
Caught within the fractured light.
In these shards, a world revealed,
Nature's magic, unsealed.

From dusk till dawn, they intertwine,
Waves of colors softly shine.
In the fractures, hope ignites,
Guiding hearts through darkened nights.

Dreams on the Breeze

Whispers carried on the air,
Secrets hidden everywhere.
The world unfolds in gentle sighs,
Where wishes dance and laughter flies.

Petals float on unseen streams,
Caught in the web of our dreams.
Each heartbeat melding with the night,
In every shadow, love takes flight.

Stars convene in twilight's breath,
Moments grasped before their death.
In the stillness, hopes arise,
Drifting softly through the skies.

Clouds cradle the stories told,
Weaving warmth through nights so cold.
In the spaces in between,
Life's essence glimmers, bright and keen.

As dawn approaches, dreams will sway,
In the dawn and fading gray.
On the breeze, our spirits soar,
Embracing life forevermore.

Silken Mists

In dawn's embrace, the mists arise,
Veiling the world in soft disguise.
Whispers of dreams upon the stream,
A floating tapestry of a waking dream.

Pale tendrils dance through emerald glades,
Softening edges of the sunlit shades.
Each breath a secret, gently spun,
In the silken mists, all time is one.

Echoes of longing in the cool, crisp air,
Each note a promise, delicate and rare.
The heart sways gently, caught in the tide,
Lost in the beauty where stillness hides.

Yet shadows linger where light does fray,
Ghostly reminders that fade away.
In this realm of whispers, I find my truth,
In silken mists, I reclaim my youth.

With every step, the world unfolds,
A story woven, yet untold.
In the gentle breath of morning's kiss,
I wander freely in the silken mist.

Labyrinth of Breath

In the maze where silence dwells,
A tapestry of untold spells.
Each inhale a map, each exhale a way,
Through the labyrinth where shadows play.

Walls of whispers, soft and deep,
Guarding secrets we dare not keep.
Every turn holds a chance to find,
The echoes of our tangled mind.

Faint footprints guide on paths unknown,
With every breath, new seeds are sown.
Inhale the light, exhale the strife,
Navigating the currents of life.

A flicker of doubt, a spark of grace,
In the winding paths, we find our place.
Through winding routes, we push and tug,
In the labyrinth of breath, we free the hug.

Whispers of solace linger near,
Each heartbeat a message, crystal clear.
In the tangled depths, I seek my worth,
In the labyrinth of breath, I find my birth.

Prismatic Echo

Fragments of light in a fleeting dance,
Colors collide at a glance.
Every hue tells a different tale,
In the prismatic echo, we sail.

Reflections of laughter, shadows of tears,
Memories woven across the years.
In the spectrum bright, we weave and spin,
In each vibrant color, we begin.

A flicker of orange, a ripple of blue,
In the kaleidoscope, we are new.
Each tone a heartbeat, pulsing and bold,
In the prismatic echo, we unfold.

The world spins round in chromatic blaze,
Life's dance a canvas, a vibrant craze.
Every moment a brushstroke fine,
In the prism's embrace, our spirits shine.

As twilight descends, the colors blend,
A symphony painted, a journey to send.
In the quiet dusk, our dreams ignite,
In the prismatic echo, we find our light.

Whirlwind of Hues

Colors collide in a wild embrace,
Creating a tempest, a brilliant space.
A whirlwind of hues spins and twirls,
In this vibrant storm, imagination unfurls.

Fuchsia and gold, a radiant clash,
Brush strokes of madness in a brilliant flash.
Spirals of laughter, cascades of glee,
In the whirlwind of hues, we are free.

Through swirls of emerald, glimmers of wine,
A tapestry woven, a dance so divine.
Every tilt and flare, unbound and bright,
In the cyclone of colors, we ignite.

Chaos and beauty intertwined,
In the whirlwind's heart, our souls aligned.
We spin like dervishes, lost in the game,
In this vibrant tempest, we find our name.

As the echoes fade, and stillness reigns,
A canvas remains, with vibrant stains.
In the whirlwind of hues, forever we'll roam,
Creating our art, making the world our home.

Luminous Whirl

In the depths of the night sky,
Stars begin to swirl and dance,
Whispers of light begin to fly,
In an enchanting, cosmic trance.

Galaxies spin, a radiant sight,
Echoes of beauty, vast and wide,
In this luminous dream of light,
Where shadows and bright worlds collide.

Time stands still in the warm glow,
Mysteries wrapped in a twirl,
In the silence, secrets flow,
In this luminous whirl.

Colors burst in the twilight,
A symphony of hues astound,
Transforming the dark into bright,
Making a magic all around.

Embrace the night, let it serve,
As the stars weave their gentle yarn,
In this twinkling, endless curve,
A celestial dance, an eternal dawn.

Veil of Sparkles

A veil of sparkles drapes the air,
In shimmering trails, they play and roam,
A gentle touch, a whisper rare,
Guiding the lost ones back to home.

Each twinkle tells a quiet tale,
Of dreams once spun in tender night,
Where wishes take a daring sail,
With every glint, they shine so bright.

In twilight's grasp, the world awakes,
To hues of silver, gold, and blue,
While softly through the silence breaks,
The hope that breathes in skies anew.

Wrap me in this delicate glow,
With your sparkles, let me fly,
In the embrace of dreams that flow,
I find my heart beneath the sky.

Underneath the vast expanse,
With stardust woven in my seams,
I take a leap, I lose my chance,
Yet find myself in fragile dreams.

Shimmering Horizons

Across the sea, the colors blend,
With waves that dance in morning light,
The horizon meets its glowing friend,
In a tapestry of day and night.

Whispers of change fill the air,
As sunbeams paint the sky in gold,
Every glance, a promise to share,
Stories of warmth that never grow old.

The shimmering light calls out to me,
Guiding my steps to the unknown,
Each step I take, I feel more free,
In this realm where dreams are sown.

Painted skies, with hues untamed,
Where the ocean meets the land,
In this dance, my heart is named,
By the beauty of nature's hand.

Together we chase the fading sun,
In moments crafted, sheer delight,
Hand in hand, 'til day is done,
In shimmering horizons, holding tight.

Threads of Radiance

Threads of radiance weave the dawn,
A tapestry of hopes and dreams,
In the morning light, we are drawn,
To the magic sewn in gentle beams.

Each thread carries whispers bold,
Stories of love that sparkle and gleam,
In vibrant colors, marvels unfold,
Embracing the heart, igniting the dream.

Woven whispers of the night,
Knit with care, they find their way,
Guiding souls, in search of light,
Through the shadows of night and day.

With every stitch, life is made whole,
In patterns of laughter, tears, and sighs,
A fabric rich, with every roll,
Crafting the moments where hope flies.

So take these threads, hold them near,
In your hands, let the stories flow,
With every knot, release the fear,
In threads of radiance, love will grow.

Chasing Shadows of Radiance

In the dusk where dreams collide,
Softly glow the fading light.
Each shadow whispers secrets low,
As stars prepare for night's embrace.

Fractured beams on silver streams,
They dance like thoughts, elusive, free.
We chase them through the quiet night,
In search of what we long to see.

With every step, the whispers grow,
Painting visions in the dark.
They lead us through the forest deep,
Where hope ignites a tiny spark.

And as the dawn begins to break,
The shadows fade, our journey ends.
Yet in our hearts, they leave a trace,
Of radiance that never bends.

The Magic of Transparent Days

In morning light, the world awakes,
With colors pure, a crisp delight.
Each raindrop holds a universe,
Where every glance can spark a flight.

Through open windows, breezes sigh,
They carry tales of skies and dreams.
The magic hums in every breath,
As sunlight weaves through silver beams.

Moments linger, soft and bright,
As laughter dances in the air.
Transparent days, a fleeting gift,
They remind us of the joy to share.

With every heartbeat, stories grow,
In each embrace, the world feels light.
A tapestry of life unfolds,
In the embrace of day's sweet might.

Echoes of Luminescent Whispers

Beneath the moon, the world sleeps soft,
Where shadows play and secrets tend.
Echoes rise from depths unknown,
In silence, whispers gently blend.

Every breeze carries a tale,
Of dreams entwined in starlit nights.
Luminescent whispers, clear and bright,
They guide us through the fleeting sights.

Between the stars, a melody,
Of hopes and wishes, softly spun.
Each moment holds a fragrant breath,
As night unveils what dreams have won.

We walk through realms of twilight grace,
In the embrace of cosmic flow.
The echoes linger, rich and warm,
In every heart, their stories grow.

The Subtle Art of Weightless Beauty

In every leaf that sways on high,
A dance unfolds, both soft and sweet.
The subtle art made clear in time,
Where beauty finds its lightest feat.

With gentle touch, the colors blend,
As petals fall and rise anew.
In fragile grace, the world unfolds,
Revealing wonders through and through.

Silent moments, breaths held tight,
They wrap the day in velvet hue.
The weight of silence speaks in tones,
Of love and loss, of old and new.

As twilight whispers soft goodbyes,
We find the beauty in the near.
The art of weightless, fleeting moments,
Exists within, forever clear.

Bubbles of Luster

Round and bright they dance in air,
Floating freely without care,
Colors burst with fleeting grace,
Joyful moments we embrace.

Each one carries a wish untold,
Captured dreams of young and old,
With a pop they fade away,
Leaving traces of a day.

Sparkling joy, a perfect scene,
Children laugh, pure and serene,
In their laughter, life ignites,
Chasing shadows into light.

Fragile forms, they drift and sway,
In the breeze, they softly play,
Nature's art in hazy hue,
Moments cherished, fresh as dew.

Bubbles rise and gently fall,
In their glory, we stand tall,
For in the dance of fleeting bliss,
We find magic in the mist.

Ephemeral Reflections

Mirrors of the fleeting skies,
Rippling waves where truth resides,
Glimmers caught in twilight's hold,
Stories whispered, gently told.

Each wave breaks upon the shore,
Carrying secrets, forevermore,
Fading echoes of the past,
Rippling memories that hold fast.

In stillness, every thought appears,
Reflected hopes, and hidden fears,
Gently swirling in the stream,
A dance of life, a waking dream.

Nature's canvas, softly drawn,
Paints a tale that lingers on,
Though the moment swiftly fades,
In the heart, the beauty wades.

Ephemeral, yet never lost,
In the silence, we embrace the cost,
For every ripple fades away,
But in our souls, they ever stay.

Starlit Exhalation

In the night, the stars ignite,
A cosmic dance of pure delight,
Whispers of the universe,
Breathe the magic, softly converse.

Every twinkle tells a tale,
Of distant worlds beyond the pale,
In their glow, our dreams take flight,
Guided by the quiet light.

Celestial bodies, a timeless sight,
Filling darkness with their might,
Each exhale a spark divine,
Drawing hearts with threads that twine.

In the silence of the night,
Close your eyes, hold on tight,
For in the starlit, cosmic sea,
Lies the essence of you and me.

Breathe and feel the universe,
In this dance, we all immerse,
Each starlit breath, a gift to share,
In the calm, we are laid bare.

Vivid Breath of Dawn

Awakening in hues of gold,
Nature's palette, bright and bold,
Each ray kisses the sleeping earth,
Celebrating a new day's birth.

Mist hangs low upon the ground,
Silent whispers, a soothing sound,
Birds break forth in joyous flight,
Singing melodies of pure delight.

Flowers bloom with colors rare,
Unfurling petals, fragrant air,
Morning's glow, a tender brush,
Painting life in vibrant hush.

The world awakens, fresh and bright,
Chasing shadows, welcoming light,
Each moment filled with hope anew,
In the dawn, dreams come true.

Vivid breath, a symphony,
Nature's hymn, a melody,
In every heartbeat, warmth we find,
A promise of love intertwined.